MW01177829

I strive to serve God humbly with this gift He has blessed me with. I hope this book reminds you of God's grace all around us.

♡Rochelle

Eden

ROCHELLE WATT

Copyright © 2022 Rochelle Watt

All rights reserved.

ISBN: 978-1-7780863-0-4

DEDICATION

for: you

CONTENTS

Some explain creation scientifically.

Some interpret nature spiritually.

I perceive the world poetically.

"The poetry of the earth is never dead." — John Keats

ACKNOWLEDGMENTS

Thank you, Dagmar, for helping me grow as a poet and writer. Thank you for all the editing, mentorship, and inspiration.

Thank you, Anthony, for your amazing work on the cover and the media content. I'm grateful for all your support throughout this process.

Thanks to those at SIM who have encouraged me along this journey. Your prayers have been invaluable.

'Mountains Make Me Think' was first published in Ekstasis Magazine Fall 2020.

willow

what were you like in Eden?

perhaps you didn't weep,
but laughed until you cried;
until you were weak,
unable to stand up straight.

a belly-bursting,
body-shaking,
contagious laughter.

here, are you aware
of suffering?
of injustice?
do you think back to
those better days?

your falling leaves, a reminder
of God's promise
to wipe away every tear.

a sullen posture
radiating hope.

Dust to Dust

Determined to dig
our way to the centre
of the earth,

minutes became

hours became

endless joy.

Unafraid of the imperfect,
dirt and dust became
badges of honour.

Mud pies before lunch.
A castle of refuge
so a worm didn't become food.

Now, I treasure
even more things made
from dirt.

Man from the earth.

We are nothing but dust.
That should be enough to humble us.

unearthed

Bury it deep
within the woods,
beneath
fallen leaves of a tree
big enough
to consume sunlight.

Take it to a territory
untouched;
off the beaten path -
only you, nature, and God.

Many secrets
must be hidden
in forests.
The wind murmurs a mysterious tale;
animals tread cautiously.

I used to dispose of secrets there,

but now see through the facade of trust,
like bare trees in the autumn.

Nothing is covered up
that will not be revealed.
Nothing is hidden
that will not be made known.

Sahara

life is a desert.

we live through the hottest days,

coldest nights.

spilled buckets of beige paint;

a mundane existence.

endless 9 to 5s.

faint glimmers of hope glistening on the horizon.

the older we get,

dreams sometimes disappear.

we let go of optimism

for a future merely filled with mirages.

only the strong survive.

like cacti.

reminded why I need to have deep roots

in times of drought.

faith that soaks up truths from God.

storing them up for future use.

what are you so afraid of?

faced head on,
fog easily dissolves.
it is weak,
not hard to overcome.

near the ground,
mysterious -
deep angst.

in the sky,
a cloud -
lovely.

a lesson
in how to interpret our fears.

Ruah

unseen,
not unfelt,
a gentle embrace
soothes my skin,
ruffles my hair
like a trusted lover.
ears kissed with whispered promises.

showered with tranquility,
I imagine it carrying my worries wherever it goes.
wishing I could dance so freely to destinations unknown.

I've seen the destruction it causes,
great strength untamed.
but not tonight.
tonight, there is kindness in the air,
silently enjoying each other's company.

Ode to the Houseplant

The friend I needed
before knowing what I needed.

Wild leaves
of bed-head
on a lazy Saturday morning.

I love your
unashamed posture of independence;
with delicate
humility knowing you would perish
without my watering.

You don't know
I depend on you
as much as you depend on the water;
as much as you depend on the sun.

You make this abode cozier.
Loneliness no longer lives here.

Reading Genesis
together at dusk;
you're quiet, as usual.
Soft whispers
of oxygen into the air.
Silent expressions of your love.

Mini-Me

if God were
a tree
we would be
bonsais

miniature
versions
of someone greater
than us

made in
His
image

to
reflect
His likeness

Anxiety: Part 1

no storehouses nor barns.
sleep never lost
in anxious worry about food.

seasons change;
time to come and go.
innocent trust
replaces questions on shelter.

sweet hymns of the birds –
their endless praise and worship.

their melody:
secretly laughing
at us?

examining our wealth and wisdom
that can't rid us of cares and concerns.

tears of stress become our food
rather than seeking the bread of life.

pillars of panic become our shelter
rather than resting in His sanctuary.

we have forgotten our worth
if we don't remember God values us
more than He does the birds.

Anxiety: Part 2

Most days, I'm a dormant volcano.

Head held high;
a noble confidence, easily earning respect.

A little smoke
shows I'm working hard.
But buried deep,

constant ebb and flow
of lava I've learned to discipline.

Sakura

If April showers
bring May flowers,
I would endure the wildest downpours
to see you bloom;

travel across an ocean with nothing
but a backpack
of hope
and pockets
bursting with anticipation.

A life expectancy
shorter than my attention span,
I've grown
with patient gratitude.

Two short weeks,
earth is transformed
into what I imagine
heaven to be.
If you are a glimpse of heaven,
please sign me up   for eternity.

A Love Letter

my moon.

loneliness exchanged
for your presence
constant
on dark nights

you clothe me in courage

reminded
shadows are temporary,
often not what they seem

lighting up every room you walk into
captivating my attention fully,
others fade into the background

bold and majestic,
earning respect with quiet humility
proud to admit your glow comes from
the Son

when your splendor is not on full display,
a hazy, dim light
behind the overwhelming presence of life's troubles,
i hope to light up your darkness on those nights

Isn't it Ironic?

we watch leaves slowly die

vintage hues
are the snapshots we choose
as our landscape views
backdrop to canoes

we watch leaves slowly die

their frailty stronger
than their determination
a fatality
to the slightest breeze

we watch leaves slowly die

they dance in the wind
to the beat of their own drum
standing ovations
for their final bow

we watch leaves slowly die

we flock to forests
capturing photos of fall
foliage

and call it beautiful

autumn leaves
leave me believing
beauty is still alive in dead things

Chrysalis

Does a caterpillar know
it is destined greatness?
One day it will soar
to unimaginable heights
in delicate silky garments?
If it knew the process required
for wings of freedom
would it still risk it all?
Embrace the darkness ahead,
the other side   unknown?
Or would it remain complacently crawling?

Right now,
are you a butterfly?
Confident, glowing, unmeasurable strength -
surviving the night you were certain would crush you.

Or,
a caterpillar?
Unsure what's next,
blissful ignorance;
this is as good as it gets.

Or,
currently entrenched in the cocoon?
A situation you did not choose, reeking of death and decay;
hope left outside.

As you can't get a rainbow without the rain,
beautification surely comes after the pain.

How to Love a Stranger

"That's the most boring,
uninspiring,
unattractive
thing I've seen",
is never said
about a sunset.

We admire its colours,
sweeping across the sky;
a calming, pastel palette.
We swoon over its details;
rays romantically kissing the earth.
We long for the peace it brings
after a long day of life.

If only we saw people this way.

Maybe we would love others better
if we saw their colours,
details,
and presence
as things to be cherished and celebrated.

Butterfly Stroke

I was never a good swimmer,
but I've always loved
water.

I love the bold, thunder-clapping waves
causing my body to dance a little -
shiver.

I love the smell of chlorine
that intoxicates a pool.

The fragrance in a raindrop
on a cozy Sunday afternoon.

I love flirting with waves of summer.
Timidly approaching where water meets
sand,   toes,   legs,   back.

Tempted to turn back,
when all I want to do is dive right in.

Bone chilling first dip;
soothed back to warmth,
an engulfing embrace.

Isn't this a lot like love?

I've always loved
love,
but was never a good swimmer.

Name-calling

I love dandelions.
Droplets of sunshine on earth.

Shimmering petals
become cotton balls of feathers,
holding wishes
the wind is eager to deliver.

One of the most beautiful
plants I've seen.

"But they are weeds"

Why should
the labels
we've placed on things
determine their
beauty and significance?

Country Mouse

The sun still slumbered.
Dawn sat perched upon a star,
awaiting her cue to ring in a new morn.

Like a teenager with a secret,
I quietly got dressed in nimbleness
and snuck out the back door of the city.

The concrete jungle
became a mere mirage in my rear-view mirror,
passing cities I couldn't pronounce.
My car ran dry.
I coerced it with
promises of freshwater lakes;
syrup that runs from trees.

The city
reminds me we worship ourselves:
crafting concrete into condos that
stretch toward the heavens.
Without cell reception
our Towers of Babel quickly crumble;
no way of staying connected.

The country
reminds me God deserves worship:

He crafted nothing into beauty,
stretching toward the heavens.
Prayer,   our way of staying connected.
A reception that never dies,
because without Him we would crumble.

Mountains Make Me Think

Lord, have You made anything
More majestic than a mountain?

The most grandiose of Your creations;
I'm reminded of how small I am,

Towering so brilliantly above me
With peaks that cradle the sky and kiss the heavens.

I envy mountains because of how close they dance to the sun.
I long for the day I can dance with the Son.

Maybe that's why
Mountains make me think of You.

-

Playing peek-a-boo with a mountain
Reminds me of people who have so much more to offer than
they show.

Thick clouds wrap their droplets around a mountain's peak,
Hiding its true potential.

Only when the clouds roll away
Do you see the ice-capped crown adorning this colossal
creation.

Heavy fog at dawn makes you think
There's nothing noteworthy on the horizon.

But on a thick sheet of grey,
I can faintly make out God's brushstrokes of a rocky skyline

And my patient determination
Is no match against time.   I'll wait.

Until the weight of the fog is lifted,
Pride shifted to vulnerability.

Until there's nothing standing
Between mountain and me,

And I can see every perfect crevice
Of imperfection and still call it beautiful.

Maybe that's why
Mountains make me think of you.

-

Can God really move mountains?
"It's awfully lofty", I whisper softly.

As if I've forgotten
He rained manna from the heavens

And turned water into wine.
He made the sun stand still; split the red sea;

And I still see what I've read about
Metaphorically all around me.

Dry bones may not live
But I've seen Him breathe life into dead situations.

Maybe that's why
Mountains make me think of us.

Demure

awestruck
by the way they strike
perfect balance of wonder and fright,
of art and power

a standing ovation,
applause echoing through the air

I remain grounded,
aware that I won't always be

the brightest in the
room

A New Perspective

Stars
–

beauty to behold,
no matter how dark it gets

Constellations
–

order in the mayhem,
purpose in the seemingly messy

Shapeshifters

Laid here for so long
the grass has familiarized itself with my shape.

Blades caress my head,
hips dip into this place I now call home.

Covered by a blanket of shalom,
the wind whispers
"Stay as long as you'd like".

I couldn't leave
if I wanted to.
Captivated by the most beautiful blue,

I've become enamoured with
shapeshifters inhabiting the sky.

Oriana

Apparently, the best part of waking up
is Folgers in your cup.

Untrue for me,
my preference is tea,

and I know an experience enticing me out of bed
more than bean water or the smell of bacon.

Sleep abandoned at dawn for
a glimpse of this sweet scene.
Heart yearning for the east,
perched by the window awaiting
that cosmic peek-a-boo.

"Good morning, sun" I whisper tiredly.
"Good morning, beautiful" he whispers back.

Silver Lining

I hate winter.

Exposed skin whimpers
beneath a thousand glacial daggers.
Daylight evicted
as darkness unpacks boxes
of sadness and gloom.

> *Yet, there is something magical*
> *about snow.*

> *When you wake to a world bleached to elegance;*
> *tracks of the night replaced*
> *with a clean slate.*

> *Watching snowflakes gracefully descend,*
> *hoping God unveils*
> *the secret recipe for why no two are ever the same.*

Or why my mourning is frozen tears.
Why it appears mercy has turned her back,
migrated on the wings of a feathered nomad.

> *Those snowflakes thaw my heart*
> *to seek the good in each season.*

Christmas in July

Hot cocoa by a fire,
enthralled by the leaping flames
mimicking Nutcracker ballerinas.
Mariah Carey.
Fruit cake.
The fresh flavour of peppermint
that makes everything livelier.

Most of all,
the evergreen.
An aroma marrying pines and earth;
a crisp fragrance signaling
a hopeful season.
A time of peace.

Then time moves on.

Yet, evidence of the evergreen endures.

A pine needle safely nestled behind a couch.
Though hidden,
love, joy, hope, peace
are still present.

These things don't die –
just like the evergreen.

Hidden Memories

not how it feels between my toes.
not its softness, expanse;
the perfect setting for morning strolls.

not the imagination it ignites.
a building block for kingdoms
with castles, moats, and knights.

my favourite thing about the sand
is the nostalgia it creates;
finding it hidden and tucked away in every unlikely place.

in the car, in the bathroom,
at the bottom of my purse.
filled with joy as I reminisce
about the beaches I've traversed.

Well Lived

fleeting life
until we are nothing but a beautiful memory

one people talk about
look up to
and admire

live like a shooting star

dazzling and fierce
only for a short moment
and we don't know who's watching

Familia

the earth needs

winter;

crisp air.
a cold, bold truth
reminding me plants grow in the spring preceded by
dark days,
dormancy,
bitter temperatures.

spring;

cool showers
of tears we've cried,
excited for the blossoms they will bear.

summer;

gut-busting laughter,
long days of sunshine.
a hope offered;
glowing skin beneath beams of fresh rays.

autumn,

learning to embrace
when it's time for things to die.

better at letting go,
seeing the beauty in all the changes.

seasons;

needing each of you
as much as I need myself.

Nevaeh

all things
made new
pain and suffering,
"adieu"

creation restored
living in one accord

run with hyenas,
swim with sharks
eternal laughter
with old testament patriarchs

floral colours never fade
nature existing as it was made

no natural disasters,
death,
fear
all things in harmony

year after year

    after year after

        year after year...

Eden

Unimaginable
place where perfection resided
and
beauty birthed.

The air:
saturated with sweet gold.
Eternal blue skies,
the softest warmth.

Lamb lay with lion.
Man and beast
face to face.

The presence of God
embraced,
and His grace graced

the seen and unseen.

Here, we long for the flawless.
A blazing desire
to experience creation in its wholeness.

We wait,
eyes fixed upwards.
Forgetting,
although perfection perished,

hidden fragments of
faith, hope, and love
remain
on this side of Eden.

Manufactured by Amazon.ca
Bolton, ON

25422917R00032